ENGLISH TOWN

FOR EVERYONE

BOOK

4

Contents

Characters

Dad

Mom

Kelly

Sam

Henry

Anna

Hello Song

Hello, everyone.
Hello, teacher!
Hello, friends!

Let's have fun together.
We'll have a good time.

Are you ready to start?
We're ready!

Here we go!

Goodbye Song

Did you have fun?

It's time to say goodbye.
See you next time!
See you next time!

Did you enjoy the class?
Yes! We had a fun time!
Yes! We had a fun time!

See you later! See you later!
Goodbye. Goodbye.

♪ Bye! Bye!

Lesson 1

A Day Plan

A. Look, listen, and repeat.

Anna, do you have any plans today?

No, I don't.

Why don't we go to a folk village?

No, I don't want to.

Henry, do you have any plans today?

No, I don't.

Why don't we go to the Global Village Festival?

That's a good idea.

ACT IT OUT

No, I don't.

6

B. Listen and practice.

Why don't we go to a folk village?

① folk village   ② festival   ③ fair   ④ concert

C. Listen, point, and say.

A: Why don't we go to a festival?
B: That's a good idea.

A. Listen and chant.

Do you have any plans today?
No, I don't. No, I don't.
Why don't we go to a fair?
No, I don't want to.
Why don't we go to a festival?
No, I don't want to.
Why don't we go to a concert?
No, I don't want to.
Why don't we go to a folk village?
That's a good idea!

B. Read and choose.

ⓐ Why don't we go to a concert?

ⓑ Why don't we go to a fair?

ⓒ Why don't we go to a festival?

ⓓ Do you have any plans today?

C. Match, ask, and answer.

A: Why don't we go to a folk village?
B: That's a good idea.

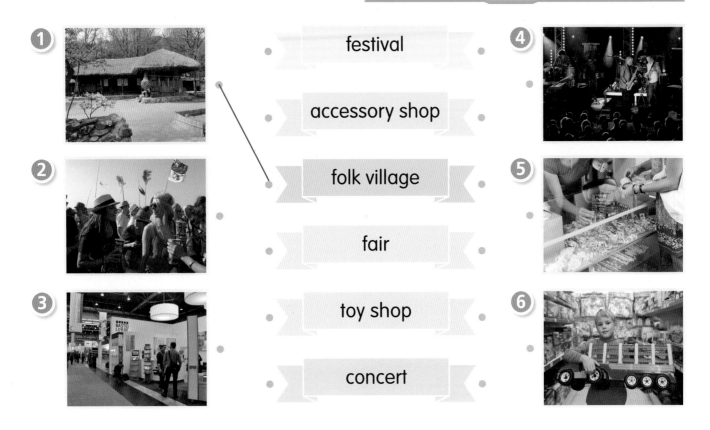

1
festival

accessory shop

folk village

fair

toy shop

concert

4

5

6

D. Work with your friends.

- Where do you want to go with your friends? Draw and ask your friends.

Why don't we go to a folk village?

No, I don't want to.

Name		Yes	No
Name		Yes	No

Transportation

Let's Talk

A. Look, listen, and repeat.

Henry, hurry up.

I'm coming.

It takes thirty minutes by subway.

How long does it take by subway?

Anna, hurry up!

I'm coming.

How long does it take by taxi?

It takes twenty minutes by taxi.

ACT IT OUT

I'm coming.

B. Listen and practice.

How long does it take by subway?

① by subway ② by taxi ③ by car ④ by train

A: How long does it take by train?
B: It takes thirty minutes by train.

C. Listen, point, and say.

① thirty ② ten ③ ten ④ twenty

A. Listen and chant.

Hurry up! Okay.

Hurry up! Okay.

How, how, how long does it take by subway?

It takes thirty minutes. It takes thirty minutes.

How, how, how long does it take by car?

It takes twenty minutes. It takes twenty minutes.

Let's go! Let's go!

B. Listen and number.

e-learning

C. Match, ask, and answer.

> A: How long does it take by subway?
> B: It takes an hour by subway.

①

②

③

by subway

by train

by plane

by taxi

by bus

by car

④

⑤

⑥

D. Work with your friends.

- Where do you often go? How do you get there and how long does it take?
  Write and talk with your friends.

> How long does it take by subway?

> It takes twenty minutes by subway.

	Where	How	How long
You		by _____	_____ minutes
Your Friend		by _____	_____ minutes

Lesson 3 Why Don't We Go to the Global Village Festival?

A. Listen and repeat.

B. Listen and number the pictures.

14

Leo Lola Nick Popo

I'm coming.

Popo, hurry up!

Oh, no!

How long does it take by taxi?

It takes 20 minutes by taxi.

C. Read and circle.

1 Where are they going?
- They are going to the (Global Village Festival, amusement park).

2 How long does it take by taxi?
- It takes (fifteen, twenty) minutes by taxi.

D. Choose the place you want to go on Sunday and do a role-play.

A. Listen and sing.

Let's Go to a Festival

Do you have any plans today?
　No, I don't. No, I don't.
Do you have any plans today?
　No, I don't. No!
Why don't we go to a festival?
　That's a good idea! That's a good idea!
How long does it take by bus?
　It takes thirty minutes by bus.
Hurry up! Hurry up!
　Okay. Okay.

B. Play a board game.

♥ Why don't we ...?
★ How long ...?
♣ It takes ... .

Transportation

One of the oldest types of transportation is the boat. Sea traders set out in small boats to trade their goods with other people thousands of years ago. Today, ships still use old sea trade routes. In some parts of the world, people travel mostly by walking or by riding animals such as donkeys, horses, and camels.

Today, flying is the most popular way to travel long distances. Can you believe that over half a million people are in the air at any time?

It takes thirteen hours by plane.

Check It Out!

1. What animals do people ride as transportation?
2. What is the most popular way to travel long distances?

Countries

Let's Talk

A. Look, listen, and repeat.

Let's go to that booth.

No way! Why don't we go there?

Anna, what country do you want to learn about?

I want to learn about the Philippines.

Let's go to the Philippines booth.

No, I don't want to! Why don't we go there?

What country do you want to learn about?

I want to learn about France.

ACT IT OUT

Let's go to that booth.

18

B. Listen and practice.

I want to learn about the Philippines.

① the Philippines ② Mongolia ③ Kenya ④ the USA

C. Listen, point, and say.

A: What country do you want to learn about?
B: I want to learn about Mongolia.

A. Listen and chant.

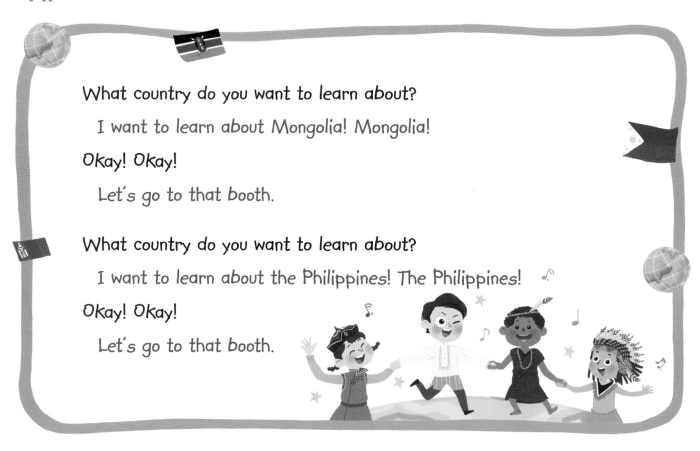

What country do you want to learn about?

I want to learn about Mongolia! Mongolia!

Okay! Okay!

Let's go to that booth.

What country do you want to learn about?

I want to learn about the Philippines! The Philippines!

Okay! Okay!

Let's go to that booth.

B. Listen and number.

ⓐ

ⓑ

ⓒ

ⓓ

C. Match, ask, and answer.

> A: What country do you want to learn about?
> B: I want to learn about the Philippines.

1

2

3

| Mongolia | the USA | the Philippines | Japan | Kenya | France |

4

5

6

D. Work with your friends.

- What country do you want to learn about? Write and ask your friends.

You

1. _____

2. _____

3. _____

Your Friend

1. _____

2. _____

3. _____

> What country do you want to learn about?

> I want to learn about Mongolia.

France

Let's Talk

A. Look, listen, and repeat.

Excuse me. What is France famous for?

France is famous for art.

Isn't it the *Mona Lisa*?

Yes, it is.

Mom, what is France famous for?

France is famous for food.

Yes, it is.

Isn't it a baguette?

ACT IT OUT

What is France famous for?

22

B. Listen and practice.

Isn't it a baguette?

① baguette ② cheese ③ olive oil ④ lobster

C. Listen, point, and say.

A: Isn't it a baguette?
B: Yes, it is.

Let's Learn

A. Listen and chant.

Isn't it the *Mona Lisa*?

Yes, it is. Yes, it is.

What is France famous for?

The Eiffel, the Eiffel, the Eiffel Tower.

Wow! Great! It looks great!

Isn't it a baguette?

Yes, it is. Yes, it is.

What is France famous for?

Baguettes! Cheese! So many foods!

Wow! Yummy! It looks yummy!

B. Read and check.

① Isn't it a baguette? ?

☐ Yes, it is. ☐ No, it isn't.

② ? Yes, it is.

☐ Isn't it cheese? ☐ Do you like cheese?

③ Isn't it a lobster? ?

☐ Yes, it is. ☐ No, it isn't.

④ What is France famous for? France ?

☐ Yes, it is. ☐ France is famous for food.

e-learning

C. Go down the ladder.
Then, ask and answer.

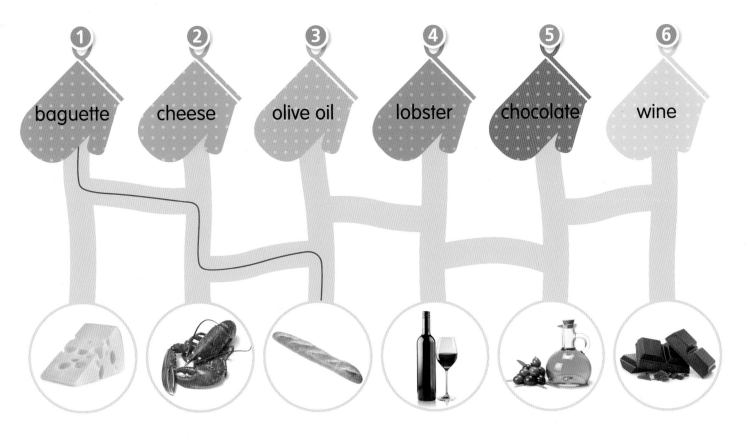

A: Isn't it a baguette?
B: Yes, it is.

1 baguette 2 cheese 3 olive oil 4 lobster 5 chocolate 6 wine

D. Work with your friends.

- Draw your favorite food and have your friends guess what it is.

Isn't it pizza?

Yes, it is!

Isn't It Cheese?

A. Listen and repeat.

B. Listen and number the pictures.

C. Read and check True or False.

1. France is famous for clothes. .... True ☐ False ☐

2. Lola  wants to learn about France. .... True ☐ False ☐

3. A mouse  took cheese from the table. .... True ☐ False ☐

D. Choose the country you want to learn about and do a role-play.

 ☐  ☐  ☐

Let's Play

A. Listen and sing.

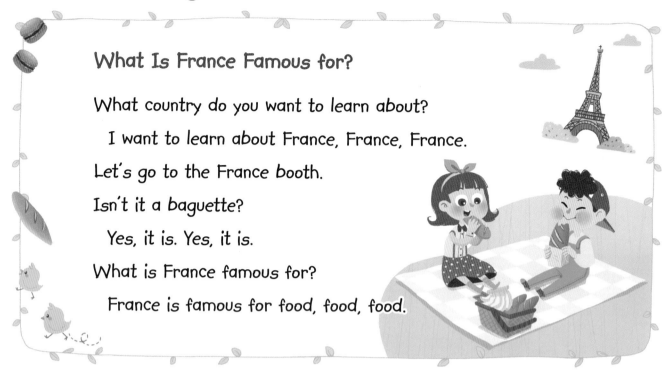

What Is France Famous for?

What country do you want to learn about?

I want to learn about France, France, France.

Let's go to the France booth.

Isn't it a baguette?

Yes, it is. Yes, it is.

What is France famous for?

France is famous for food, food, food.

B. Play a game. Spin a pencil!

(art)

(food)

SCORE

You	Your Friend

♥ What country do you want to learn about?

★ Isn't it a lobster?

♣ What is France famous for?

e-learning

The Eiffel Tower

It is in Paris. It was built as the entrance arch for the 1889 World Fair. It was named after engineer Gustave Eiffel. His company designed and built the tower in 1889. It took 2 years, 2 months, and 5 days to build the tower. The tower is 324 meters tall. When it was built, it was the tallest building in the world.

At that time, the French people didn't like the design and wanted to demolish it. But today it is the most-visited monument in the world.

I want to learn about France.

Check It Out!

1. When was the Eiffel Tower built?
2. Did the French people like the Eiffel Tower at first? Why?

Lesson 7

Houses

Let's Talk

A. Look, listen, and repeat.

Look at this picture!

A house is in the tree.

Excuse me? Is this a tree house?

Yes. Some people live in tree houses.

Laos

Look at this picture!

A house is on the water.

Excuse me? Is this a floating house?

Yes. Some people live in floating houses.

Cambodia

ACT IT OUT

Look at this picture!

B. Listen and practice.

Is this a tree house?

① tree house

② floating house

③ tent

④ igloo

C. Listen, point, and say.

A: Is this a tree house?
B: Yes. Some people live in tree houses.

Let's Learn

A. Listen and chant.

Look! Look! Look at this picture!
Wow! A house is in the tree.
Is this a tree house?
Yes! Yes! Some people live in tree houses.

Look! Look! Look at this picture!
Wow! A house is on the water.
Is this a floating house?
Yes! Yes! Some people live in floating houses.

B. Read and choose.

①

②

③

④

ⓐ Some people live in tents.

ⓑ Some people live in floating houses.

ⓒ Some people live in tree houses.

ⓓ Some people live in igloos.

C. Ask and answer.

A: Is this a tree house?
B: Yes. Some people live in tree houses.

①
tree house(s)

②
floating house(s)

③
tent(s)

④
igloo(s)

⑤
log house(s)

⑥
townhouse(s)

D. Work with your friends.

- Look, match, and talk with your friends.

Is this a tree house?

Yes. Some people live in tree houses.

Lesson 8 — Market Places

A. Look, listen, and repeat.

How interesting!

Yes, it is.

They are selling fruit on the boat.

What are they doing?

Yes, it is.

How interesting!

What are they doing?

They are selling food on the street.

Act It Out

Yes, it is.

B. Listen and practice.

They are selling fruit on the boat.

1
fruit,
on the boat

2
food,
on the street

3
clothes,
in the garage

4
ice cream,
in the van

C. Listen, point, and say.

A: What are they doing?
B: They are selling fruit on the boat.

Let's Learn

A. Listen and chant.

How interesting!
How interesting!
Yes, it is. Yes, it is.
What are they doing?
What are they doing?
They are selling fruit on the boat, on the boat.
What are they doing?
What are they doing?
They are selling food on the street, on the street.

B. Listen and number.

ⓐ

ⓑ

ⓒ

ⓓ

C. Ask and answer.

A: What are they doing?
B: They are selling fruit on the boat.

1

fruit, on the boat

2

food, on the street

3

clothes, in the garage

4

ice cream,
in the van

5

things,
at the flea market

6

lemonade,
at the park

D. Work with your friends.

- Draw the things you want to sell and talk with your friends.

What are they doing?

They are selling orange juice in the van.

on the street

in the van

in the garage

on the boat

Lesson 9

How Interesting!

Look at this!

A house is in the tree!

Is this an igloo?

Yes. Some people live in igloos.

A. Listen and repeat.

B. Listen and number the pictures.

How ...!

C. Read and circle.

1 Where are Nick, Popo, Leo, and Lola?

- They are in (a tent, **an igloo**).

2 What are Leo and Lola doing?

- They are (selling ice cream, **chasing a mouse**).

D. Where do they live? What are they doing? Choose and do a role-play.

A. Listen and sing.

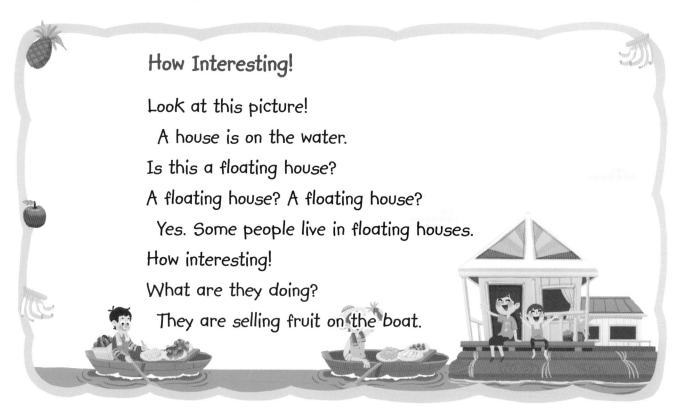

How Interesting!

Look at this picture!
  A house is on the water.
Is this a floating house?
A floating house? A floating house?
  Yes. Some people live in floating houses.
How interesting!
What are they doing?
  They are selling fruit on the boat.

B. Play a board game.

START

Is this a _____?

They are selling fruit _____.

Is this an _____?

They are selling clothes _____.

Is this a _____?

Back to Start

Is this a _____?

They are selling ice cream _____.

FINISH

Igloos

In very cold places, igloos are common. An igloo is a house made out of snow. It protects people from extreme conditions. This house is specially made by people who live in very cold climates. They are called *Inuits*.

An igloo is made of snow or ice, but the temperature inside can range from -7°C to 16°C even if the temperature outside is -45°C or so.

Some people live in igloos.

Check It Out!

1. What is an igloo made of?
2. Would you like to live in an igloo? Why or why not?

Assessment Test 1

1. Listening

A. Listen and check.

1

a. ☐
b. ☐

2

a. ☐
b. ☐

3

a. ☐
b. ☐

4

a. ☐
b. ☐

5

a. ☐
b. ☐

6

a. ☐
b. ☐

B. Listen and answer the questions.

1 Where will they go?
   a. They will go to a concert.
   b. They will go to a festival.
   c. They will go to a fair.

2 What country does Tom want to learn about?
   a. the Philippines   b. France   c. Spain

2. Speaking

A. Look, listen, and reply.

1

2

3

4

ten

B. Number the sentences in order and talk with your partner.

◯ Why don't we go to a festival?

① Do you have any plans today?

◯ No, I don't.

◯ That's a good idea.

A. Read and match.

1 Is this an igloo?   •   • a. That's a good idea.

2 Why don't we go to   •   • b. I'm coming.
   a concert?

3 What are they doing? •   • c. It takes 10 minutes by car.

4 Hurry up!   •   • d. Yes. Some people live in igloos.

5 How long does it take •   • e. I want to learn about Mongolia.
   by car?

6 What country do you •   • f. They are selling ice cream
   want to learn about?   in the van.

B. Read and check True or False.

Ryan: Katie, let's go to the France booth.
Katie: No, I don't want to. I want to learn about the Philippines.
Ryan: Then, let's go to the Philippines booth.
Katie: Look at this picture. A house is on the water.
Ryan: Excuse me. Is this a floating house?
Staff: Yes. Some people live in floating houses.
Ryan: How interesting!
Katie: Yes, it is.

1 Katie wants to learn about France. .... True ☐ False ☐

2 Katie and Ryan went to the Philippines booth. .... True ☐ False ☐

3 Katie and Ryan are interested in the floating house. ... True ☐ False ☐

4. Writing

e-learning

> by taxi   floating house   folk village   lobster
> baguette   on the street   the Philippines

A. Write the words.

1

_____

2

_____

3

_____

4

_____

5

They are selling food

_____ .

6

It takes ten minutes

_____ .

7

Isn't it a _____?

B. Write the answers.

1 Henry: How long does it take by subway?
Mom: _____
(by / takes / subway / it / thirty / minutes /.)

2 Anna: What are they doing?
Staff: _____
(selling / on / they / fruit / the / boat / are /.)

3 Dad: What country do you want to learn about?
Anna: _____
(about / I / to / USA / the / learn / want /.)

Mongolia & Spain 1

Let's Talk

A. Look, listen, and repeat.

How big is Mongolia?

It's bigger than the Philippines.

Where is Mongolia?

It's in Asia.

ASIA

How big is Spain?

It's smaller than France.

Where is Spain?

It's in Europe.

EUROPE

ACT IT OUT

How big is Mongolia?

B. Listen and practice.

It's in Asia.

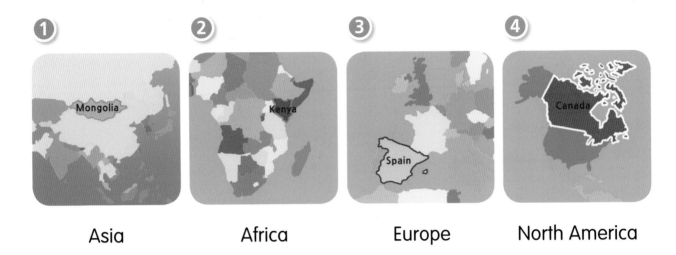

① Asia   ② Africa   ③ Europe   ④ North America

A: Where is Canada?
B: It's in North America.

C. Listen, point, and say.

A. Listen and chant.

How, how, how big is Mongolia?
Bigger, bigger, it's bigger than the Philippines.
Where, where, where is Mongolia?
Asia, Asia, it's in Asia.

How, how, how big is Spain?
Smaller, smaller, it's smaller than France.
Where, where, where is Spain?
Europe, Europe, it's in Europe.

B. Read and choose.

1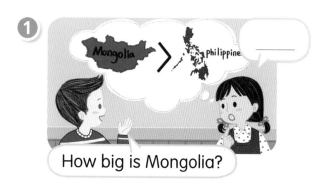

How big is Mongolia?

2

It's in Asia.

3

Where is Spain?

4

It's smaller than France.

ⓐ It's bigger than the Philippines.

ⓑ How big is Spain?

ⓒ Where is Mongolia?

ⓓ It's in Europe.

C. Ask, answer, and check.

> A: Where is Mongolia?
> B: It's in Asia.

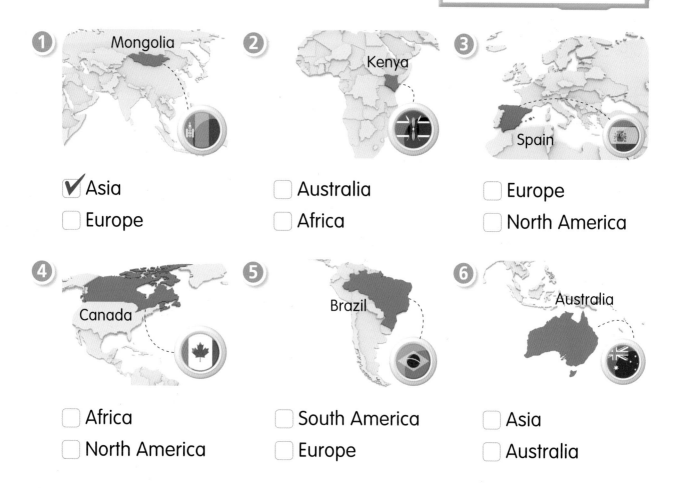

1 Mongolia
- ✔ Asia
- ☐ Europe

2 Kenya
- ☐ Australia
- ☐ Africa

3 Spain
- ☐ Europe
- ☐ North America

4 Canada
- ☐ Africa
- ☐ North America

5 Brazil
- ☐ South America
- ☐ Europe

6 Australia
- ☐ Asia
- ☐ Australia

D. Work with your friends.

- Write your favorite countries and talk with your friends.

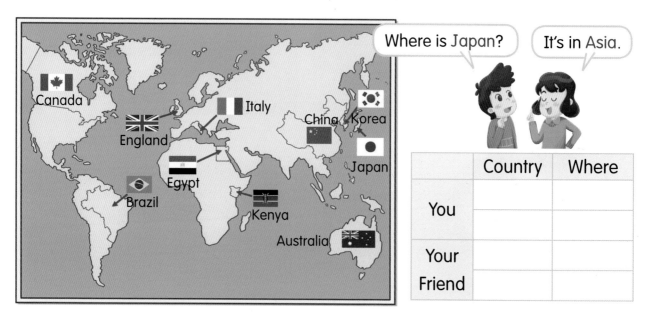

> Where is Japan?
> It's in Asia.

	Country	Where
You		
Your Friend		

Lesson 12

Mongolia & Spain 2

Let's Talk

A. Look, listen, and repeat.

How far is Mongolia?

It's far. It takes about three hours.

3hrs

What can I do in Mongolia?

You can ride a horse.

How far is Spain?

It's very far. It takes about thirteen hours.

13hrs

What can I do in Spain?

You can dance the flamenco.

ACT IT OUT

How far is Mongolia?

B. Listen and practice.

You can ride a horse.

①

②

③

④

ride a horse

dance the
flamenco

sleep in the
desert

see a bullfight

C. Listen, point, and say.

A: What can I do in Spain?
B: You can dance the flamenco.

A. Listen and chant.

Mongolia! Mongolia! How far is it?

It's far. It's far.

It takes three hours, three hours!

What can I do in Mongolia?

You can ride a horse. Sounds great!

Spain! Spain! How far is it?

It's very far. It's very far.

It takes thirteen hours, thirteen hours!

What can I do in Spain?

You can dance the flamenco. Sounds great!

B. Listen and number.

a

b

c

d

C. Ask and answer.

A: What can I do in Mongolia?
B: You can ride a horse.

1

Mongolia,
ride a horse

2

Spain,
dance the flamenco

3

Mongolia,
sleep in the desert

4

Spain,
see a bullfight

5

the USA,
watch a baseball game

6

France,
eat a baguette

D. Work with your friends.

- Write the country you want to visit and draw what you can do there. And talk with your friends.

I want to visit _____.

What can I do in Australia?

You can see many kangaroos.

Leo and Lola Are in Space

Where is Spain?

It's in Europe.

How big is Spain?

It's bigger than Italy.

A. Listen and repeat.

B. Listen and number the pictures.

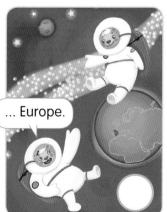

... Europe.

How big ...?

C. **Read and circle.**

① How big is Spain?

- It's bigger than (France, Italy).

② What can I do in Spain?

- You can (dance the flamenco, sleep in the desert).

D. **Choose the country you want to visit and do a role-play.**

A. Listen and sing.

Where Is Mongolia?

Where is Mongolia?

It's in Asia. It's in Asia.

What can I do in Mongolia?

You can ride a horse. You can ride a horse.

Where is Spain?

It's in Europe. It's in Europe.

What can I do in Spain?

You can dance the flamenco. You can dance the flamenco.

B. Play a board game.

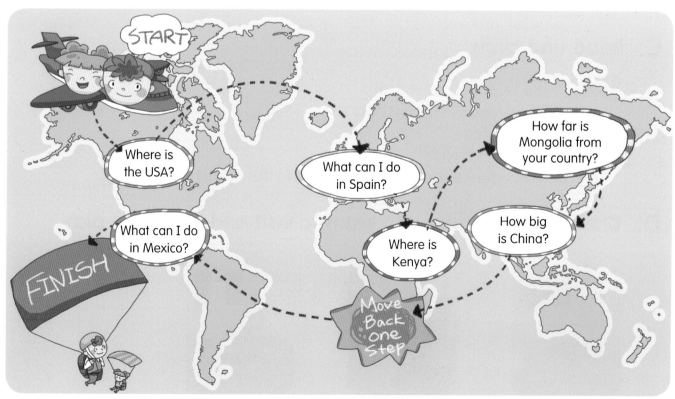

e-learning

Oceans and Continents

The planet Earth is a huge ball with both land and water on its surface. As it is a ball, we can only see one side of the Earth at a time. But we can stretch out the surface to get a map that looks like this one.

Arctic Ocean

ASIA

NORTH
AMERICA

PACIFIC
OCEAN

ATLANTIC
OCEAN

AFRICA

INDIAN OCEAN

PACIFIC
OCEAN

SOUTH
AMERICA

AUSTRALIA

Southern Ocean

ANTARCTICA

The Earth's water splits into five large bodies that are called oceans. Their names are the Pacific Ocean, the Atlantic Ocean, the Indian Ocean, the Southern Ocean, and the Arctic Ocean. The Earth's land is divided into seven areas that are called continents. Their names are Asia, Africa, North America, South America, Antarctica, Europe, and Australia.

Check It Out!

1. How many oceans are there in the world?
2. How many continents are there in the world?

Lesson 14 Traditional Costumes

Let's Talk

A. Look, listen, and repeat.

Wow, what are all these?

These are *hanbok*.

Excuse me. Can you tell me about it?

It's a Korean wig.

Excuse me. What are all these?

These are Mongolian costumes.

Can you tell me about them?

They're Mongolian boots.

ACT IT OUT

Wow, what are all these?

B. Listen and practice.

It's / They're a Korean wig.

① a Korean wig   ② Mongolian boots   ③ a Chinese mask   ④ a Mexican hat

C. Listen, point, and say.

A: Can you tell me about it / them?
B: It's / They're a Korean wig.

A. Listen and chant.

What are all these? What are all these?

They're boots! They're boots!

Can you tell me about them?

Mongolian boots! Mongolian boots! They're Mongolian boots!

Wow, what is this? What is this?

It's a mask! It's a mask!

Can you tell me about it?

A Chinese mask! A Chinese mask! It's a Chinese mask!

B. Listen and number.

a

b

c

d

C. Match, ask, and answer.

A: Can you tell me about them?
B: They're Korean wigs.

①

Korean wigs

Chinese masks

④

②

Mexican hats

Mongolian boots

⑤

③

Arab turbans

Scottish kilts

⑥

D. Work with your friends.

- Draw the things you want to sell and talk with your friends.

You

Can you tell me about them?

They're Chinese masks.

Describing People

Let's Talk

A. Look, listen, and repeat.

B. Listen and practice.

You look like a queen.

① queen ② king ③ princess ④ prince

C. Listen, point, and say.

A: How do I look?
B: You look like a king.

A. Listen and chant.

Hey, hey!
How do I look?
You look like a queen!
May I take a picture?
Sure! Sure! Of course!

Hey, hey!
How do I look?
You look like a king!
May I take a picture?
Sure! Sure! Of course!

B. Read and choose.

1. _____
2. _____
3. _____
4. _____

a) You look like a prince.

b) You look like a princess.

c) You look like a king.

d) You look like a queen.

C. Go down the ladder.
   Then, ask and answer.

A: How do I look?
B: You look like a queen.

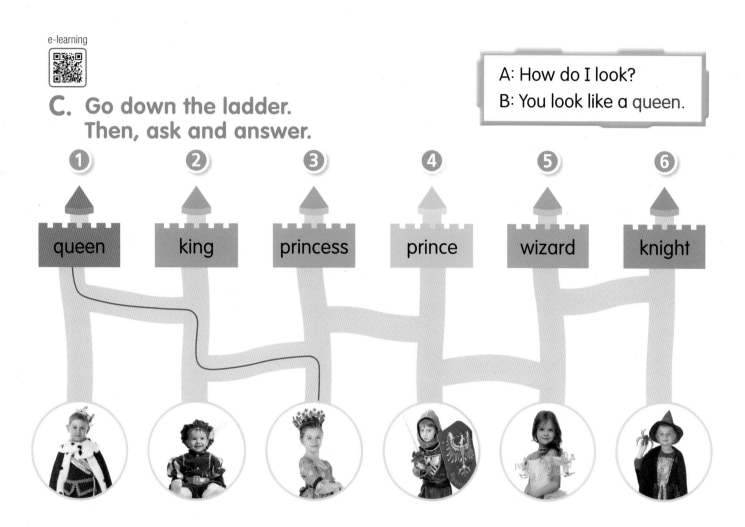

D. Work with your friends.

- Draw yourself and ask your friends how you look.

How do I look?   You look like a prince.

You Look Great!

These are *hanbok*.

Wow! What are all these?

You look great!

Thank you.

A. Listen and repeat.

B. Listen and number the pictures.

Thank you.

66

C. Read and circle.

1. What is Lola wearing?
   - She is wearing (*hanbok*, Mongolian boots).

2. How does Popo look?
   - He looks like a (prince, princess).

D. What would you like to try on? Choose and do a role-play.

A. Listen and sing.

How Do I Look?

Wow! Wow! What are all these?
   These are *hanbok*. These are *hanbok*.
Wow! Wow! They are so beautiful!
Can you tell me about it?
   It's a Korean wig. It's a Korean wig.
May I take a picture?
   Of course. Of course.
How do I look?
   You look like a prince. You look like a queen.

B. Play a game. Spin a pencil!

♥ What are all these?
★ Can you tell me about it [them]?
♣ How do I look?

e-learning

Traditional Clothes around the World

In India, many women wear saris. A sari is a large piece of cloth. A person can wear it like a skirt, veil, or head cover.

The ao dai is Vietnam's national costume for women. Young girls usually wear white, and unmarried women wear pastels. Married women wear rich-colored tops with simple black or white pants.

The kilt is a traditional Scottish item of clothing for men. Usually knee length, this piece of cloth is wrapped around men's hips and legs. It's famous for its checkered designs.

Check It Out!

1. Who wears saris?
2. What's the name of Vietnam's national costume for women?
3. What is a kilt?

A Campaign for Poor Children

Lesson 17

Let's Talk

A. Look, listen, and repeat.

Mom! Dad! Look at these babies.

Oh... they look so sick.

Why are they so sick?

Because they don't have warm clothes.

Dad! Look at these children.

Oh... they look so sick.

Why are they so sick?

Because they don't have enough food.

Oh… they look so sick.

B. **Listen and practice.**

Because they don't have warm clothes.

① warm clothes ② enough food ③ clean water ④ enough medicine

C. **Listen, point, and say.**

A: Why are they so sick?
B: Because they don't have clean water.

Let's Learn

A. Listen and chant.

Mom! Dad! Look at these children.
Mom! Dad! Look at these children.
Oh, oh… they look so sick.
Why, why, why are they so sick?
Because they don't have warm clothes.
Why, why, why are they so sick?
Because they don't have enough food.

B. Read and choose.

1 Why are they so sick?

2

3

4

a Because they don't have enough medicine.　**b** Because they don't have warm clothes.

c Because they don't have clean water.　**d** Because they don't have enough food.

C. Ask and answer.

> A: Why are they so sick?
> B: Because they don't have warm clothes.

1 warm clothes

2 enough food

3 clean water

4 enough medicine

5 safe homes

6 good nurses and doctors

D. Work with your friends.

- Think and draw the things they need. And talk with your friends.

Why are they so sick?

Because they don't have clean water.

Draw

Draw

Helping Children

Let's Talk

A. Look, listen, and repeat.

Mom, what do they need?

They need wool hats.

What should we do for them?

We should knit a hat.

Dad, what do they need?

They need clean water and food.

What should we do for them?

We should raise money!

ACT IT OUT

Mom, what do they need?

B. Listen and practice.

We should knit a hat.

① knit a hat   ② raise money   ③ write a letter   ④ send clothes

C. Listen, point, and say.

A: What should we do for them?
B: We should write a letter.

Let's Learn

A. Listen and chant.

What do they need? What do they need?
Wool hats! Wool hats! They need wool hats!
What should we do for them?
Knit a hat! Knit a hat! We should Knit a hat.

What do they need? What do they need?
Clean water! Enough food!
They need clean water and enough food.
What should we do for them?
Raise money! Raise money!
We should raise money for them.

B. Listen and number.

a ◯ b ◯ c ◯ d ◯

C. Match, ask, and answer.

> A: What should we do for them?
> B: We should knit a hat.

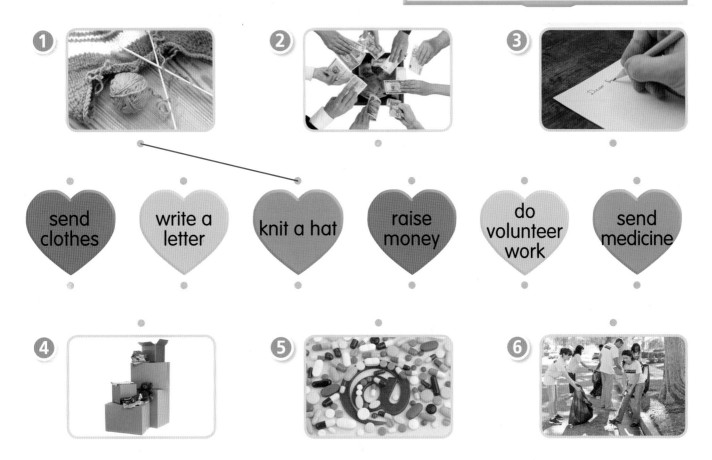

1 **2** **3**

send clothes   write a letter   knit a hat   raise money   do volunteer work   send medicine

4 **5** **6**

D. Work with your friends.

- Read, draw, and talk about what you should do for Huan.

Draw   Draw

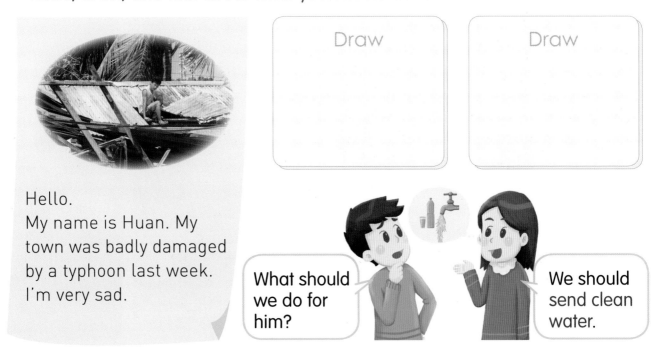

Hello.
My name is Huan. My town was badly damaged by a typhoon last week. I'm very sad.

What should we do for him?

We should send clean water.

What Should We Do for Them?

A. Listen and repeat.

B. Listen and number the pictures.

... sick?

C. Read and circle.

1 Why are the baby birds so sick?

- Because they don't have enough (water, food) and warm clothes.

2 What should Leo 🐭 and his friends do for the baby birds?

- They should (catch, eat) worms and (write a letter, knit a hat).

D. What should we do for them? Think and do a role-play.

 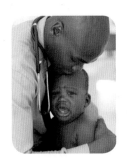 

A. Listen and sing.

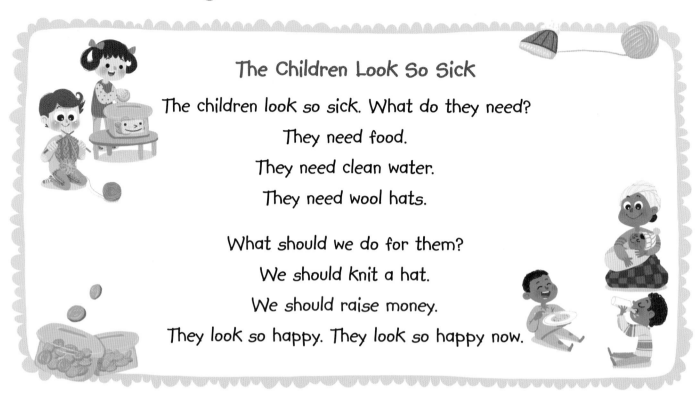

The Children Look So Sick

The children look so sick. What do they need?

They need food.

They need clean water.

They need wool hats.

What should we do for them?

We should knit a hat.

We should raise money.

They look so happy. They look so happy now.

B. Play a board game.

★ Why are they so sick?

♥ What should we do for them?

80

What Is Hats for Hunger?

Hats for Hunger is a charity. It was founded by Andrew Castle in 2008. A charity is a group of people that raises money to help poor kids.

Andrew Castle started it when he was only nine years old! He read a story about a poor kid in a catalog and wanted to help the poor children. He decided to knit hats and sell them. In 2008, Andrew, his little brother, and their mom knitted some hats. They raised $1,500 that year. In 2010, he raised $5,000, and he keeps increasing the amount he raises.

Check It Out!

1. When did Andrew start Hats for Hunger?
2. How did Andrew help poor kids?
3. How much money did Andrew and his family raise in 2008?

Lesson 20 Assessment Test 2

A. Listen and check.

①

a. ☐
b. ☐

②

a. ☐
b. ☐

③

a. ☐
b. ☐

④

a. ☐
b. ☐

⑤

a. ☐
b. ☐

⑥

a. ☐
b. ☐

B. Listen and answer the questions.

① How big is Mongolia?
  a. It's bigger than France.
  b. It's smaller than the Philippines.
  c. It's bigger than the Philippines.

② What can we do in Spain?
  a. We can see a bullfight.
  b. We can ride a horse.
  c. We can sleep in the desert.

A. Look, listen, and reply.

B. Number the sentences in order and talk with your partner.

◯   Of course. How do I look?

◯   You look like a queen.

①   May I take a picture?

A. Read and match.

1. How do I look?

2. Why are they so sick?

3. Where is Spain?

4. What should we do for them?

5. What can I do in Mongolia?

6. Can you tell me about it?

a. You can sleep in the desert.

b. We should send clothes.

c. You look like a king.

d. It's in Europe.

e. It's a Korean wig.

f. Because they don't have enough food.

B. Read and check True or False.

Amy: Dad, look at these babies.
Dad: Oh… they look so sick.
Amy: Why are they so sick?
Dad: Because they don't have warm clothes and medicine.
Amy: What should we do for them?
Dad: We should raise money.
Amy: I see. What about knitting hats for them?
Dad: That's a good idea!
Amy: Okay! I'll knit wool hats for them.

1. The babies need warm clothes and medicine. .... True ☐ False ☐

2. Amy will knit wool hats. .... True ☐ False ☐

3. Amy will send them warm clothes and medicine. ... True ☐ False ☐

write a letter   a Korean wig   enough medicine
princess   Africa   see a bullfight   a Mexican hat

A. Write the words.

①

②

③

④

_____   _____   _____   _____

⑤

⑥

⑦

We should _____ .   It's _____ .   You can _____ .

B. Write the answers.

① Henry: What should we do for them?
Mom: _____
(knit / we / should / a / hat /.)

② Anna: Why are they so sick?
Dad: _____
(they / clean / because / have / water / don't /.)

③ Henry: What can I do in Spain?
Staff: _____
(flamenco / the / you / dance / can /.)

Syllabus

	Topic	Language	Key Vocabulary
Lesson 1	A Day Plan	Why don't we go to a folk village? - That's a good idea. / No, I don't want to. Do you have any plans today? - No, I don't. / Yes, I do.	folk village festival fair concert
Lesson 2	Transportation	How long does it take by subway? - It takes thirty minutes by subway. Hurry up! - I'm coming.	by subway by taxi by car by train
Lesson 3	Why Don't We Go to the Global Village Festival?	Step Up 1 (Review Lessons 1-2) ∗Reading Time: Transportation	
Lesson 4	Countries	What county do you want to learn about? - I want to learn about the Philippines. Let's go to that booth. - No way! Why don't we go there?	the Philippines Mongolia Kenya the USA
Lesson 5	France	Isn't it the *Mona Lisa*? - Yes, it is. / No, it isn't. What is France famous for? - France is famous for art[food].	baguette cheese olive oil lobster
Lesson 6	Isn't It Cheese?	Step Up 2 (Review Lessons 4-5) ∗Reading Time: The Eiffel Tower	
Lesson 7	Houses	Is this a tree house? - Yes. Some people live in tree houses. Look at this picture! - A house is in the tree.	tree house floating house tent igloo
Lesson 8	Market Places	What are they doing? - They are selling fruit on the boat. How interesting! - Yes, it is.	fruit, on the boat food, on the street clothes, in the garage ice cream, in the van
Lesson 9	How Interesting!	Step Up 3 (Review Lessons 7-8) ∗Reading Time: Igloos	
Lesson 10	Assessment Test 1 (Review Lessons 1-9)		

	Topic	Language	Key Vocabulary
Lesson 11	Mongolia & Spain 1	Where is Mongolia? - It's in Asia. How big is Mongolia? - It's bigger than the Philippines.	Asia Africa Europe North America
Lesson 12	Mongolia & Spain 2	What can I do in Mongolia? - You can ride a horse. How far is Mongolia? - It's far. It takes about three hours.	ride a horse dance the flamenco sleep in the desert see a bullfight
Lesson 13	Leo and Lola Are in Space	Step Up 4 (Review Lessons 11-12) *Reading Time: Oceans and Continents	
Lesson 14	Traditional Costumes	Excuse me. Can you tell me about it [them]? - It's [They're] a Korean wig. Wow, what are all these? - These are *hanbok*.	a Korean wig Mongolian boots a Chinese mask a Mexican hat
Lesson 15	Describing People	How do I look? - You look like a queen. May I take a picture? - Of course.	queen king princess prince
Lesson 16	You Look Great!	Step Up 5 (Review Lessons 14-15) *Reading Time: Traditional Clothes around the World	
Lesson 17	A Campaign for Poor Children	Why are they so sick? - Because they don't have warm clothes. Look at these babies. - Oh… they look so sick.	warm clothes clean water enough food enough medicine
Lesson 18	Helping Children	What should we do for them? - We should knit a hat. What do they need? - They need wool hats.	knit a hat raise money write a letter send clothes
Lesson 19	What Should We Do for Them?	Step Up 6 (Review Lessons 17-18) *Reading Time: What is Hats for Hunger?	
Lesson 20	Assessment Test 2 (Review Lessons 11-19)		

Flashcard List

folk village		festival		fair	
concert		by subway		by taxi	
by car		by train		the Philippines	
Mongolia		Kenya		the USA	
baguette		cheese		olive oil	
lobster		tree house		floating house	
tent		igloo		fruit, on the boat	
food, on the street		clothes, in the garage		ice cream, in the van	
Asia		Africa		Europe	
North America		ride a horse		dance the flamenco	
sleep in the desert		see a bullfight		a Korean wig	
Mongolian boots		a Chinese mask		a Mexican hat	
queen		king		princess	
prince		warm clothes		enough food	
clean water		enough medicine		knit a hat	
raise money		write a letter		send clothes	

Lesson 1 A Day Plan

	Vocabulary	Meaning	Sentence
1	folk village*	민속촌	Why don't we go to a folk village?
2	festival*	축제	Why don't we go to a festival?
3	fair*	박람회	Why don't we go to a fair?
4	concert*	연주회, 콘서트	Why don't we go to a concert?
5	accessory shop*	액세서리 가게	Why don't we go to an accessory shop?
6	toy shop*	장난감 가게	Why don't we go to a toy shop?
7	any	어느, 어떤	Do you have any plans today?
8	plan	계획	Do you have any plans today?
9	today	오늘	Do you have any plans today?
10	want	원하다	No, I don't want to.
11	idea	생각	That's a good idea.
12	global village	지구촌, 다문화	Why don't we go to the Global Village Festival?

Lesson 2 Transportation

	Vocabulary	Meaning	Sentence
1	by subway*	지하철로	How long does it take by subway?
2	by taxi*	택시로	How long does it take by taxi?
3	by car*	자동차로	How long does it take by car?
4	by train*	기차로	How long does it take by train?
5	by bus*	버스로	How long does it take by bus?
6	by plane*	비행기로	How long does it take by plane?
7	hurry	서두르다	Hurry up!
8	minute	분	It takes thirty minutes by subway.
9	twenty	20	It takes twenty minutes by taxi.
10	thirty	30	It takes thirty minutes by subway.
11	How long ~?	(시간, 길이 등이) 얼마나	How long does it take by subway?
12	take	(시간이) 걸리다	How long does it take by car?

Lesson 5 France

	Vocabulary	Meaning	Sentence
1	baguette*	바게트(빵)	Isn't it a baguette?
2	cheese*	치즈	Isn't it cheese?
3	olive oil*	올리브 오일	Isn't it olive oil?
4	lobster*	바닷가재	Isn't it a lobster?
5	chocolate*	초콜릿	Isn't it chocolate?
6	wine*	와인	Isn't it wine?
7	Mona Lisa	모나리자	Isn't it the Mona Lisa?
8	France	프랑스	What is France famous for?
9	art	미술, 예술	France is famous for art.
10	food	음식, 식품	France is famous for food.
11	famous	유명한	What is France famous for?
12	famous for	~으로 유명한	France is famous for food.

Lesson 6 Isn't It Cheese?

	Vocabulary	Meaning	Sentence
1	clothes	옷, 의복	France is famous for clothes.
2	mouse	쥐	A mouse took cheese from the table.
3	took	(take의 과거형) 가지고 갔다	A mouse took cheese from the table.
4	table	식탁, 탁자	A mouse took cheese from the table.
5	wait	기다리다	Wait!
6	come back	돌아오다[가다]	Come back here!
7	entrance	입구	It was built as the entrance arch for the World Fair.
8	engineer	엔지니어, 기술자	It was named after engineer Gustave Eiffel.
9	tower	탑	His company designed and built the tower in 1889.
10	build	세우다, 짓다	It took about 2 years to build the tower.
11	demolish	붕괴시키다	The French people wanted to demolish it.
12	monument	기념비	It is the most-visited monument in the world.

Lesson 3 — Why Don't We Go to the Global Village Festival?

	Vocabulary	Meaning	Sentence
1	amusement park	놀이공원	Why don't we go to the amusement park?
2	transportation	운송[교통] 수단	One of the oldest types of transportation is the boat.
3	boat	배	One of the oldest types of transportation is the boat.
4	trade	거래[무역/교역]하다	Sea traders set out in small boats to trade their goods.
5	goods	물건, 상품	Sea traders set out in small boats to trade their goods.
6	travel	여행하다	People travel mostly by walking.
7	walking	걷기	People travel by walking.
8	donkey	당나귀	People travel by riding donkeys and camels.
9	camel	낙타	People travel by riding donkeys and camels.
10	flying	항공[비행기] 여행, 비행	Flying is the most popular way to travel long distances.
11	popular	인기 있는	Flying is the most popular way to travel long distances.
12	distance	거리	Flying is the most popular way to travel long distances.

Lesson 4 — Countries

	Vocabulary	Meaning	Sentence
1	the Philippines*	필리핀	Let's go to the Philippines booth.
2	Mongolia*	몽골	I want to learn about Mongolia.
3	Kenya*	케냐	I want to learn about Kenya.
4	the USA*	미국	I want to learn about the USA.
5	Japan*	일본	I want to learn about Japan.
6	France*	프랑스	I want to learn about France.
7	let's	(함께) ~하자	Let's go to that booth.
8	booth	(칸막이를 한) 작은 공간, 부스	Let's go to that booth.
9	there	저곳에, 저쪽으로	Why don't we go there?
10	country	국가, 나라	What country do you want to learn about?
11	learn	배우다, 알다	What country do you want to learn about?
12	about	~에 대해 [관해]	What country do you want to learn about?

Lesson 7 — Houses

	Vocabulary	Meaning	Sentence
1	tree house*	나무 위의 집	Is this a tree house?
2	floating house*	수상 가옥	Is this a floating house?
3	tent*	텐트, 천막	Is this a tent?
4	igloo*	이글루(얼음집)	Is this an igloo?
5	log house*	통나무집	Is this a log house?
6	townhouse*	도시 주택, 연립 주택	Is this a townhouse?
7	house	집	A house is in the tree.
8	in	~ (안)에	A house is in the tree.
9	on	~ (위)에, ~의 표면에	A house is on the water.
10	some	약간의, 몇몇의	Some people live in tree houses.
11	people	사람들	Some people live in tents.
12	live	살다	Some people live in igloos.

Lesson 8 — Market Places

	Vocabulary	Meaning	Sentence
1	fruit*	과일	They are selling fruit on the boat.
2	food*	음식, 식품	They are selling food on the street.
3	clothes*	옷	They are selling clothes in the garage.
4	ice cream*	아이스크림	They are selling ice cream in the van.
5	thing*	물건	They are selling things at the flea market.
6	lemonade*	레모네이드 (레몬 탄산음료)	They are selling lemonade at the park.
7	on the boat	배 위에서	They are selling fruit on the boat.
8	on the street	거리에서	They are selling food on the street.
9	in the garage	차고에서	They are selling clothes in the garage.
10	in the van	밴에서	They are selling ice cream in the van.
11	at the flea market	벼룩시장에서	They are selling things at the flea market.
12	at the park*	공원에서	They are selling lemonade at the park.

Lesson 9 — How Interesting!

	Vocabulary	Meaning	Sentence
1	chase	뒤쫓다	They are chasing a mouse.
2	sell	팔다	They are selling ice cream in the van.
3	interesting	흥미로운	How interesting!
4	common	흔한, 일반적인	In very cold places, igloos are common.
5	protect	보호하다	It protects people from extreme conditions.
6	extreme	극한의	It protects people from extreme conditions.
7	condition	조건, 환경	It protects people from extreme conditions.
8	climate	기후	This house is made by people who live in very cold climates.
9	igloo	이글루, 얼음집	An igloo is made of snow or ice.
10	ice	얼음	An igloo is made of snow or ice.
11	temperature	온도, 기온	The temperature inside can range from -7℃ to 16℃.
12	range	(범위가) ~에서 …에 이르다	The temperature inside can range from -7℃ to 16℃.

Lesson 11 — Mongolia & Spain 1

	Vocabulary	Meaning	Sentence
1	Asia*	아시아	It's in Asia.
2	Africa*	아프리카	It's in Africa.
3	Europe*	유럽	It's in Europe.
4	North America*	북아메리카	It's in North America.
5	South America*	남아메리카	It's in South America.
6	Australia*	오스트레일리아 (대륙), 호주	It's in Australia.
7	bigger	더 큰	It's bigger than the Philippines.
8	than	~보다	It's bigger than the Philippines.
9	where	어디에, 어디로	Where is Mongolia?
10	Spain	스페인	How big is Spain?
11	smaller	더 작은	It's smaller than France.
12	Canada	캐나다	Where is Canada?

Lesson 14 — Traditional Costumes

	Vocabulary	Meaning	Sentence
1	Korean wig*	한국의 가체	It's a Korean wig.
2	Mongolian boots*	몽골 부츠	They're Mongolian boots.
3	Chinese mask*	중국 가면	It's a Chinese mask.
4	Mexican hat*	멕시코 모자	It's a Mexican hat.
5	Scottish kilt*	스코틀랜드 킬트	They're Scottish kilts.
6	Arab turban*	아랍 터번	They're Arab turbans.
7	all	모든, 모두	What are all these?
8	these	(this의 복수) 이것들	What are all these?
9	costume	(특정지역,시대의) 의상, 복장	They're Mongolian costumes.
10	tell	말하다	Can you tell me about it?
11	me	(I의 목적격) 나에게	Can you tell me about it?
12	them	(they의 목적격) 그(것)들을[에게]	Can you tell me about them?

Lesson 15 — Describing People

	Vocabulary	Meaning	Sentence
1	queen*	여왕	You look like a queen.
2	king*	왕	You look like a king.
3	princess*	공주	You look like a princess.
4	prince*	왕자	You look like a prince.
5	wizard*	마법사	You look like a wizard.
6	knight*	기사	You look like a knight.
7	May I ~?	(제가) ~해도 될까요?	May I take a picture?
8	take a picture	사진을 찍다	May I take a picture?
9	look like	~처럼 보이다	You look like a king.
10	look	~해 보이다	How do I look?
11	like	~처럼	You look like a king.
12	of course	물론, 그럼	Of course.

Lesson 12 — Mongolia & Spain 2

	Vocabulary	Meaning	Sentence
1	ride a horse*	말을 타다	You can ride a horse.
2	dance the flamenco*	플라멩코를 추다	You can dance the flamenco.
3	sleep in the desert*	사막에서 자다	You can sleep in the desert.
4	see a bullfight*	투우경기를 관람하다	You can see a bullfight.
5	watch a baseball game*	야구경기를 보다	You can watch a baseball game.
6	eat a baguette*	바게트를 먹다	You can eat a baguette.
7	far	멀리	How far is Mongolia?
8	about	약, ~쯤	It takes about three hours.
9	hour	시간	It takes about three hours.
10	thirteen	13	It takes about thirteen hours.
11	can	~할 수 있다	You can dance the flamenco.
12	many	많은	You can see many kangaroos.

Lesson 13 — Leo and Lola Are in Space

	Vocabulary	Meaning	Sentence
1	space	우주	Leo and Lola are in space.
2	Italy	이탈리아	It's bigger than Italy.
3	Mexico	멕시코	What can I do in Mexico?
4	China	중국	How big is China?
5	planet	행성	The planet Earth is a huge ball with land and water.
6	Earth	지구	The plant Earth is a huge ball with land and water.
7	huge	거대한	The planet Earth is a huge ball with land and water.
8	surface	표면	The Earth is a huge ball with water on its surface.
9	map	지도	We can stretch out the surface to get a map.
10	split	나뉘다	The Earth's water splits into five bodies called oceans.
11	ocean	대양, 바다	The Earth's water splits into five bodies called oceans.
12	continent	대륙	The land is divided into seven areas called continents.

Lesson 16 — You Look Great!

	Vocabulary	Meaning	Sentence
1	thank	감사하다, 고마워하다	Thank you.
2	great	멋진, 훌륭한	You look great!
3	beautiful	아름다운	They are so beautiful.
4	women	(woman의 복수) 여자들	In India, many women wear saris.
5	wear	입다	In India, many women wear saris.
6	cloth	옷감, 천	A sari is a large piece of cloth.
7	veil	베일, 면사포	A person can wear it like a skirt, veil, or head cover.
8	costume	의상, 복장	It is Vietnam's national costume for women.
9	pants	바지	Married women wear rich-colored tops with simple black or white pants.
10	clothing	옷, 의복	The kilt is a traditional Scottish item of clothing for men.
11	men	(man의 복수) 남자들	The kilt is a traditional Scottish item of clothing for men.
12	wrap	싸다	It is wrapped around men's hips and legs.

Lesson 17 — A Campaign for Poor Children

	Vocabulary	Meaning	Sentence
1	warm clothes*	따뜻한 옷	Because they don't have warm clothes.
2	enough food*	충분한 음식	Because they don't have enough food.
3	clean water*	깨끗한 물	Because they don't have clean water.
4	enough medicine*	충분한 약, 약물	Because they don't have enough medicine.
5	safe homes*	안전한 집(가정)	Because they don't have safe homes.
6	good nurses and doctors*	훌륭한 간호사들과 의사들	Because they don't have good nurses and doctors.
7	babies	(baby의 복수형) 아기들	Look at these babies.
8	look	~해 보이다	They look so sick.
9	so	너무나, 대단히	They look so sick.
10	sick	아픈	They look so sick.
11	why	왜	Why are they so sick?
12	because	~ 때문에, ~이니까	Because they don't have warm clothes.

Lesson 18 — Helping Children

	Vocabulary	Meaning	Sentence
1	knit a hat*	모자를 뜨다	We should knit a hat.
2	raise money*	돈을 모으다	We should raise money.
3	write a letter*	편지를 쓰다	We should write a letter.
4	send clothes*	옷을 보내다	We should send clothes.
5	send medicine *	약을 보내다	We should send medicine.
6	do volunteer work*	자원 봉사를 하다	We should do volunteer work.
7	need	필요로 하다	What do they need?
8	wool hat	털모자	They need wool hats.
9	should	～해야 한다	What should we do for them?
10	badly	심하게	My town was badly damaged by a typhoon.
11	be damaged	피해를 입다	My town was badly damaged by a typhoon.
12	typhoon	태풍	My town was badly damaged by a typhoon.

Lesson 19 — What Should We Do for Them?

	Vocabulary	Meaning	Sentence
1	worm	벌레	They need worms and wool hats.
2	baby bird	새끼 새	Why are the baby birds so sick?
3	catch	잡다	We should catch worms.
4	happy	행복한	They look so happy.
5	charity	자선 단체	A charity is a group of people that raises money to help poor kids.
6	help	도와주다	A charity is a group of people that raises money to help poor kids.
7	read	읽다	He read a story about a poor kid in a catalog.
8	poor	가난한, 불쌍한	He read a story about a poor kid in a catalog.
9	decide	결정하다	He decided to knit hats and sell them.
10	knit	뜨개질하다	He decided to knit hats and sell them.
11	increase	증가하다, 늘다	He keeps increasing the amount he raises.
12	amount	총액, 양	He keeps increasing the amount he raises.

 **Memo**

 **Memo**

Answers

Student Book
Answers

Lesson 1 A Day Plan
B. Read and choose.   p. 8
1. ⓒ   2. ⓑ   3. ⓓ   4. ⓐ

C. Match, ask, and answer.   p. 9

Lesson 2 Transportation
B. Listen and number.   p. 12
a. 4   b. 1   c. 3   d. 2

C. Match, ask, and answer.   p. 13

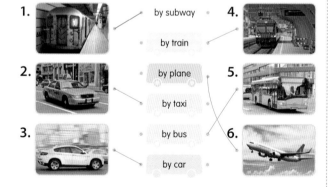

Lesson 3 Why Don't We Go to the Global Village Festival?
B. Listen and number the pictures.   p. 14

C. Read and circle.   p. 15
1. Global Village Festival   2. twenty

Reading Time   p. 17
1. People ride animals such as donkeys, horses, and camels.
2. Flying is the most popular way to travel long distances.

Lesson 4 Countries
B. Listen and number.   p. 20
a. 2   b. 4   c. 3   d. 1

C. Match, ask, and answer.   p. 21

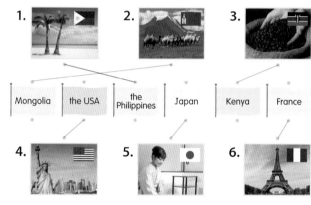

Lesson 5 France
B. Read and check.   p. 24
1. No, it isn't.   2. Isn't it cheese?
3. Yes, it is.   4. France is famous for food.

C. Go down the ladder. Then, ask and answer.   p. 25

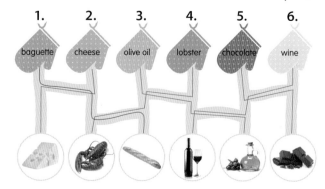

Lesson 6 Isn't It Cheese?
B. Listen and number the pictures.   p. 26

C. Read and check True or False.   p. 27

1. False   2. True   3. True

Reading Time   p. 29

1. It was built in 1889.

2. They didn't like it because they didn't like the design.

Lesson 7 Houses
B. Read and choose.   p. 32

1. ⓒ   2. ⓓ   3. ⓐ   4. ⓑ

D. Work with your friends.   p. 33

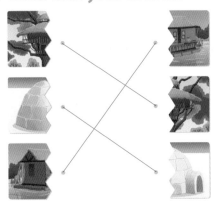

Lesson 8 Market Places
B. Listen and number.   p. 36

a. 3   b. 1   c. 4   d. 2

Lesson 9 How Interesting!
B. Listen and number the pictures.   p. 38

C. Read and circle.   p. 39

1. an igloo   2. chasing a mouse

Reading Time   p. 41

1. It is made of snow or ice.

2. [Example] I would like to live in an igloo because I want to know how it feels to live there.

Lesson 10 Assessment Test 1
Listening   p. 42

A. 1. a   2. a   3. b   4. a   5. b   6. b

B. 1. c   2. b

Speaking   p. 43

A. 1. Yes, it is.

2. Yes. Some people live in tree houses.

3. They are selling clothes in the garage.

4. It takes 10 minutes by subway.

B. ③ Why don't we go to a festival?

② No, I don't.

④ That's a good idea.

Reading   p. 44

A. 1. d   2. a   3. f   4. b   5. c   6. e

B. 1. False   2. True   3. True

Writing   p. 45

A. 1. floating house   2. baguette

3. the Philippines   4. folk village

5. on the street   6. by taxi

7. lobster

B. 1. It takes thirty minutes by subway.

2. They are selling fruit on the boat.

3. I want to learn about the USA.

Lesson 11 Mongolia & Spain 1
B. Read and choose.   p. 48

1. ⓐ   2. ⓒ   3. ⓓ   4. ⓑ

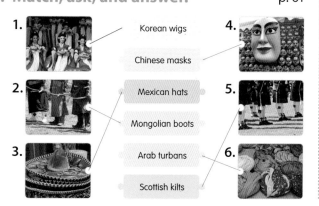

C. Match, ask, and answer. p. 77

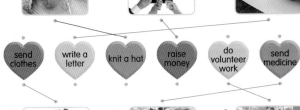

Lesson 19 What Should We Do for Them?

B. Listen and number the pictures. p. 78

C. Read and circle. p. 79
1. food   2. catch, knit a hat

Reading Time p. 81
1. He started it in 2008 when he was nine years old.
2. He raised money by knitting hats and selling them.
3. They raised $1,500 that year.

Lesson 20 Assessment Test 2

Listening p. 82
A. 1. b   2. a   3. a   4. b   5. a   6. b

B. 1. c   2. a

Speaking p. 83
A. 1. They're Mongolian boots.
2. Because they don't have warm clothes.
3. We should raise money.
4. You can dance the flamenco.

B. ② Of course. How do I look?
③ You look like a queen.

Reading p. 84
A. 1. c   2. f   3. d   4. b   5. a   6. e

B. 1. True   2. True   3. False

Writing p. 85
A. 1. enough medicine   2. princess
3. a Korean wig   4. Africa
5. write a letter   6. a Mexican hat
7. see a bullfight

B. 1. We should knit a hat.
2. Because they don't have clean water.
3. You can dance the flamenco.

Workbook
Answers

Lesson 1 A Day Plan — pp. 4~5

A. 1. Anna, do you have any plans today?
2. Why don't we go to a folk village?
3. No, I don't.
4. That's a good idea.

B. 1. fair　　　2. festival
3. concert　　4. folk village

C. 1. plans　　2. don't
3. Why　　　4. good

D. 1. Why, a festival, good idea
2. Why don't we, a fair, a good idea

Lesson 2 Transportation — pp. 6~7

A. 1. Henry, hurry up!
2. How long does it take by subway?
3. I'm coming.
4. It takes twenty minutes by taxi.

B. 1. by subway　　2. by taxi
3. by car　　　　4. by train

C. 1. Hurry　　2. coming
3. long　　　4. minutes

D. 1. How long, subway, by subway
2. How long, by taxi, It takes, by taxi

Lesson 3 Why Don't We Go to the Global Village Festival? — pp. 8~9

A. 1. plans, No　　2. idea
3. hurry　　　　4. by taxi

B. 1. Do you have any plans today?
2. Why don't we go to a concert?
3. That's a good idea!
4. It takes twenty minutes by car.

Reading Time-Voca
1. flying　　2. walking
3. travel　　4. transportation
5. boat　　　6. trade

Lesson 4 Countries — pp. 10~11

A. 1. No way! Why don't we go there?
2. What country do you want to learn about?
3. Let's go to the Philippines booth.
4. I want to learn about France.

B. 1. Mongolia　　2. the Philippines
3. the USA　　　4. Kenya

C. 1. booth　　2. No
3. country　　4. France

D. 1. country, about, learn, Mongolia
2. What country, learn about, learn about the Philippines

Lesson 5 France — pp. 12~13

A. 1. France is famous for art.
2. Isn't it the *Mona Lisa*?
3. Mom, what is France famous for?
4. Yes, it is.

B. 1. baguette　　2. cheese
3. olive oil　　4. lobster

C. 1. France　　2. food
3. olive oil　　4. Yes

D. 1. cheese, Yes, is　　2. it a lobster, Yes, it is

Lesson 6 Isn't It Cheese? — pp. 14~15

A. 1. booth　　2. France
3. lobster　　4. famous
5. cheese

B. **1.** Let's go to that booth.

    2. I want to learn about Kenya.

    3. Isn't it a baguette?

    4. France is famous for art.

Reading Time-Voca

    1. tower   **2.** monument   **3.** build

    4. demolish   **5.** engineer   **6.** entrance

Lesson 7 Houses pp. 16~17

A. **1.** Look at this picture!

    2. Yes. Some people live in tree houses.

    3. A house is on the water.

    4. Is this a floating house?

B. **1.** tree house   **2.** floating house

    3. tent   **4.** igloo

C. **1.** at   **2.** in

    3. tree house   **4.** live

D. **1.** an igloo, in igloos

    2. this a tent, live in tents

Lesson 8 Market Places pp. 18~19

A. **1.** Yes, it is.

    2. What are they doing?

    3. How interesting!

    4. They are selling food on the street.

B. **2.** food, on the street

    3. fruit, on the boat

    4. clothes, in the garage

C. **1.** How   **2.** Yes

    3. doing   **4.** on the boat

D. **1.** are, doing, are selling, on the street

    2. are they doing, are selling clothes in the garage

Lesson 9 How Interesting! pp. 20~21

A. **1.** house   **2.** igloos

    3. interesting   **4.** in the van

    5. mouse

B. **1.** A house is on the water.

    2. Some people live in floating houses.

    3. How interesting!

    4. They are selling fruit on the boat.

Reading Time-Voca

    1. ice   **2.** igloo

    3. extreme   **4.** cold

    5. temperature   **6.** protect

Lesson 11 Mongolia & Spain 1 pp. 22~23

A. **1.** It's bigger than the Philippines.

    2. Where is Mongolia?

    3. How big is Spain?

    4. It's in Europe.

B. **1.** Asia   **2.** Africa

    3. Europe   **4.** North America

C. **1.** big   **2.** smaller

    3. Where   **4.** Europe

D. **1.** Kenya, in Africa

    2. Where, Spain, in Europe

Lesson 12 Mongolia & Spain 2 pp. 24~25

A. **1.** It's far. It takes about three hours.

    2. You can ride a horse.

    3. How far is Spain?

    4. What can I do in Spain?

B. 1. ride a horse

2. dance the flamenco

3. sleep in the desert

4. see a bullfight

C. 1. far   2. takes

3. Spain   4. dance

D. 1. do, Spain, dance the flamenco

2. can, do in Mongolia, can ride a horse

Lesson 13 Leo and Lola Are in Space

pp. 26~27

A. 1. Europe   2. bigger

3. far, by plane   4. dance the flamenco

5. Let's

B. 1. It's in Asia.

2. It's bigger than the Philippines.

3. It takes three hours by plane.

4. You can ride a horse.

Reading Time-Voca

1. huge   2. surface

3. planet   4. Earth

5. ocean   6. continent

Lesson 14 Traditional Costumes pp. 28~29

A. 1. These are *hanbok*.

2. It's a Korean wig.

3. What are all these?

4. Can you tell me about them?

B. 1. a Korean wig

2. Mongolian boots

3. a Chinese mask

4. a Mexican hat

C. 1. these   2. are

3. tell   4. Mexican hat

D. 1. tell, about it, Korean wig

2. Can, tell me, Mongolian boots

Lesson 15 Describing People

pp. 30~31

A. 1. May I take a picture?

2. How do I look?

3. Of course.

4. You look like a king.

B. 1. queen   2. king

3. princess   4. prince

C. 1. picture   2. course

3. look   4. prince

D. 1. How, look, look like

2. How do, look, You look like a

Lesson 16 You Look Great!

pp. 32~33

A. 1. look   2. these

3. May   4. a Mexican hat

5. princess

B. 1. You look great.

2. May I take a picture?

3. Can you tell me about it?

4. You look like a king.

Reading Time-Voca

1. costume   2. pants

3. veil   4. wrap

5. wear   6. cloth

Lesson 17 A Campaign for Poor Children

pp. 34~35

A. 1. Look at these babies.
2. Why are they so sick?
3. Oh... they look so sick.
4. Because they don't have enough food.

B. 1. warm clothes   2. enough food
3. clean water   4. enough medicine

C. 1. Look   2. sick
3. Why   4. warm clothes

D. 1. Why, sick, Because, medicine
2. Why are, sick, Because, enough food

Lesson 18 Helping Children

pp. 36~37

A. 1. Mom, what do they need?
2. What should we do for them?
3. They need clean water and food.
4. We should raise money.

B. 1. knit a hat   2. raise money
3. write a letter   4. send clothes

C. 1. need   2. wool hats
3. should   4. knit a hat

D. 1. should, do, should write
2. What should, do, should send clothes

Lesson 19 What Should We Do for Them?

pp. 38~39

A. 1. sick   2. enough food
3. need   4. should
5. knit a hat

B. 1. They look so sick.
2. Because they don't have enough medicine.
3. They need wool hats.
4. What should we do for them?

Reading Time-Voca
1. charity   2. knit
3. help   4. increase
5. raise   6. sell

Final Test
English Town Book 4

1. ③   2. ④   3. ③   4. ⑤   5. ④
6. ②   7. ①   8. ③   9. ③   10. ⑤
11. ④   12. ②   13. ③   14. ④   15. ②
16. ④   17. ⑤   18. ④   19. should
20. What, on

Memo

Final Test

English Town Book 4

Class	Name	Score
		/20

Part 1 - Listening

[1-2] Look, listen, and choose the correct word.

1

① ② ③ ④ ⑤

2

① ② ③ ④ ⑤

[3-4] Listen and choose the correct picture.

3
① ② ③
④ ⑤

4
① ASIA / Mongolia
② EUROPE / Spain
③ AFRICA / Kenya
④ SOUTH AMERICA / Brazil
⑤ NORTH AMERICA / USA

[5-6] Listen and choose the correct sentence.

5

① ② ③ ④ ⑤

6

① ② ③ ④ ⑤

[7-8] Listen and choose the correct picture.

7
① ② ③

8
① ② ③
④ ⑤

[9-10] Look, listen, and choose the correct answer.

9

① ② ③ ④ ⑤

10
① ② ③ ④ ⑤

Part 2 - Speaking

11 Listen and choose the wrong conversation.
① ② ③ ④ ⑤

12 Listen and choose the best response to the last sentence.
① ② ③ ④ ⑤

Final Test_English Town Book 4

[13-14] Choose the correct words for the blanks.

13

A: _____ do they need?

B: They need wool hats.

① When   ② Where   ③ What

④ How   ⑤ Why

14

A: _____

B: It's a Mexican hat.

① What are they?

② Where is Mexico?

③ What can I do in Mexico?

④ Can you tell me about it?

⑤ Do you want to wear a Mexican hat?

[15-16] Read and answer the questions.

Tom: Do you have any plans today?

Jenny: _____

Tom: Why don't we go to a fair?

Jenny: No, I don't want to. I want to go to a concert.

Tom: Sounds great! Let's go!

15 What is the correct sentence for the blank?

① Yes, I am.   ② No, I don't.

③ No, I'm not.   ④ Sure, let's go.

⑤ Today is Thursday.

16 Where will Tom and Jenny go?

① a fair   ② a festival   ③ school

④ a concert   ⑤ a library

[17-18] Read and answer the questions.

Mom: Mike, let's go to a concert.

Mike: Okay. How _____ does it take?

Mom: It takes an hour by bus.

Mike: Wow! It's far. How long does it take by subway?

Mom: It takes about 40 minutes by subway.

Mike: Then, let's take the subway!

Mom: Okay.

17 What is the correct word for the blank?

① is   ② far   ③ big

④ tall   ⑤ long

18 What is NOT true about the dialog?

① It takes 40 minutes by subway.

② Mike wants to go to a concert.

③ It takes an hour by bus.

④ Mom doesn't want to take the subway.

⑤ Mike wants to take the subway.

[19-20] Choose and write the correct words.

> of   what   how   should   on

19 A: What _____ we do for them?

B: We should send warm clothes.

20 A: _____ are they doing?

B: They are selling fruit _____ the boat.

ENGLISH TOWN

FOR EVERYONE

BOOK
4

WORKBOOK

YBM

ENGLISH TOWN

TOWN

FOR EVERYONE

BOOK
4

WORKBOOK

Contents

A Day Plan

Let's Write

A. Look, choose, and write.

1. _____
   _____

No, I don't.

2. _____

No, I don't want to.

Henry, do you have any plans today?

3. _____

Why don't we go to the Global Village Festival?

4. _____

- Why don't we go to a folk village?
- Anna, do you have any plans today?
- No, I don't.
- That's a good idea.

B. Write the words.

festival   folk village   concert   fair

1
_____

2
_____

3
_____

4
_____

C. Choose and write.

1 Anna, do you have any _____ today?

2 No, I _____ .

3 _____ don't we go to a festival?

4 That's a _____ idea.

good
plans
don't
why

D. Look and write.

Example

A: Why don't we go to a <u>folk</u> <u>village</u>?

B: That's a good <u>idea</u>.

1

A: _____ don't we go to _____ _____?

B: That's a _____ _____.

2

A: _____ _____ _____ go to _____ _____?

B: That's _____ _____ _____.

Transportation

Let's Write

A. Look, choose, and write.

1 _____

I'm coming.

It takes thirty minutes by subway.

2 _____

Anna, hurry up!

3 _____

How long does it take by taxi?

4 _____
_____

- I'm coming.
- Henry, hurry up!

- It takes twenty minutes by taxi.
- How long does it take by subway?

B. Write the words.

by taxi   by subway   by train   by car

 ①
_____

 ②
_____

 ③
_____

 ④
_____

C. Choose and write.

① _____ up!

② I'm _____ .

③ How _____ does it take by bus?

④ It takes thirty _____ by bus.

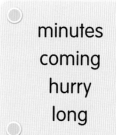

minutes
coming
hurry
long

D. Look and write.

Example

A: How long does it take _by_ _car_ ?

B: It takes thirty minutes _by_ _car_ .

①

A: _____ _____ does it take by _____ ?

B: It takes thirty minutes _____ _____ .

②

A: _____ _____ does it take _____ _____ ?

B: _____ _____ thirty minutes _____ _____ .

Why Don't We Go to the Global Village Festival?

Let's Write

A. Write the words and number the pictures.

1 Nick: Do you have any _____ today?

Popo: No, I don't.

Lola: Why don't we go to the amusement park?

Leo: _____, I don't want to.

2 Lola: Why don't we go to the Global Village Festival?

Leo, Nick and Popo: That's a good _____!

3 Nick: Popo, _____ up!

Popo: I'm coming.

4 All: Oh, no!

5 Leo: How long does it take _____?

Lola: It takes 20 minutes by taxi.

no

idea

plans

hurry

by taxi

B. Unscramble and complete the dialogs.

1 A: _____

(you / have / any / do / today / plans / ?)

B: No, I don't.

2 A: _____

(go / we / a / why / don't / to / concert / ?)

B: No, I don't want to.

3 A: Why don't we go to the Global Village Festival?

B: _____

(good / that's / idea / a / !)

4 A: How long does it take by car?

B: _____

(minutes / by / takes / twenty / it / car / .)

Reading Time – Voca

- **Write the words.**

1. _____

2. _____

3. _____

4. _____

5. _____

6. _____

trade

walking

travel

boat

flying

transportation

Countries

Let's Write

A. Look, choose, and write.

Let's go to that booth.

Spain　**Philippines**

1. _____

2. _____

I want to learn about the Philippines.

What country do you want to learn about?

3. _____

No, I don't want to! Why don't we go there?

4. _____

- I want to learn about France.
- No way! Why don't we go there?
- Let's go to the Philippines booth.
- What country do you want to learn about?

B. **Write the words.**

Mongolia   Kenya   the Philippines   the USA

1

2

3

4

_____   _____   _____   _____

C. **Choose and write.**

1 Let's go to that _____.

2 _____ way! Why don't we go there?

3 What _____ do you want to learn about?

4 I want to learn about _____.

country
no
booth
France

D. **Look and write.**

Example

A: What _country_ do you want to learn about?

B: I want to learn about _Kenya_ .

1

A: What _____ do you want to learn _____?

B: I want to _____ about _____.

2

A: _____ _____ do you want to _____

_____?

B: I want to _____ _____ _____ _____.

France

Let's Write

A. Look, choose, and write.

Excuse me. What is France famous for?

1. _____

Yes, it is.

2. _____

3. _____

France is famous for food.

Isn't it a baguette?

4. _____

- Yes, it is.
- Isn't it the *Mona Lisa*?
- France is famous for art.
- Mom, what is France famous for?

B. Write the words.

olive oil   baguette   lobster   cheese

①  _____

②  _____

③  _____

④  _____

C. Choose and write.

① What is _____ famous for?

② France is famous for _____ .

③ Isn't it _____ ?

④ _____ , it is.

France
olive oil
food
yes

D. Look and write.

Example

A: Isn't it a _baguette_ ?

B: _Yes_ , it is.

①

A: Isn't it _____ ?

B: _____ , it _____ .

②

A: Isn't _____ _____ _____ ?

B: _____ , _____ _____ .

Isn't It Cheese?

Let's Write

A. Write the words and number the pictures.

① Leo: Let's go to that _____.

Lola: No way! Why don't we go there?

② Nick: What country do you want to learn about?

Lola: I want to learn about _____.

③ Popo: Isn't it a _____?

Nick: Yes, it is.

④ Nick: What is France famous for?

Lola: France is _____ for food.

⑤ Lola: Oh, no! Isn't it _____?

Leo: Yes, it is. Wait! Come back here!

France

lobster

cheese

booth

famous

... famous for ... .

Let's ... .

B. Unscramble and complete the dialogs.

1 A: _____

(let's / booth / to / go / that / .)

B: No way! Why don't we go there?

2 A: What country do you want to learn about?

B: _____

(learn / I / to / about / want / Kenya / .)

3 A: _____

(a / isn't / baguette / it / ?)

B: Yes, it is.

4 A: What is France famous for?

B: _____

(is / for / France / famous / art / .)

Reading Time – Voca

- **Write the words.**

1. _____

2. _____

3. _____

4. _____

5. _____

6. _____

build

monument

demolish

entrance

engineer

tower

Houses

Let's Write

A. Look, choose, and write.

1. _____

A house is in the tree.

Excuse me. Is this a tree house?

2. _____
_____

Look at this picture!

3. _____

4. Excuse me. _____
_____

Yes. Some people live in floating houses.

Cambodia

- Is this a floating house?
- Look at this picture!
- Yes. Some people live in tree houses.
- A house is on the water.

16

B. Write the words.

tent   igloo   tree house   floating house

①  _____

②  _____

③  _____

④  _____

C. Choose and write.

① Look _____ this picture!

② A house is _____ the tree.

③ Is this a _____ ?

④ Yes. Some people _____ in tree houses.

in
at
live
tree house

D. Look and write.

Example

A: Is this a _tree house_ ?

B: Yes. Some people live in _tree houses_ .

①

A: Is this _____ _____ ?

B: Yes. Some people live _____ _____ .

②

A: Is _____ _____ _____ ?

B: Yes. Some people _____ _____ _____ .

Market Places

Let's Write

A. Look, choose, and write.

How interesting!

① _____

② _____
_____

They are selling fruit on the boat.

③ _____

Yes, it is.

What are they doing?

④ _____
_____

- What are they doing?
- They are selling food on the street.
- Yes, it is.
- How interesting!

18

B. Write the words.

on the boat   food   in the garage
clothes   on the street   fruit

①	②	③	④

ice cream
in the van

C. Choose and write.

① _____ interesting!

② _____, it is.

③ What are they _____?

④ They are selling fruit _____.

doing
how
yes
on the boat

D. Look and write.

Example

A: What are they _doing_?

B: They are selling fruit on the _boat_.

①

A: What _____ they _____?

B: They _____ _____ food _____ _____
_____.

②

A: What _____ _____ _____?

B: They _____ _____ _____ _____
_____ _____.

How Interesting!

Let's Write

A. Write the words and number the pictures.

① Nick: Look at this!

Popo: A _____ is in the tree.

② Nick: Is this an igloo?

Penguin: Yes. Some people live in _____.

③ Nick: How _____!

Popo: Yes, it is.

④ Nick: What are they doing?

Penguin: They are selling ice cream _____.

⑤ Penguin: What are they doing?

Nick and Popo: They are chasing a _____.

Lola and Leo: Come back!

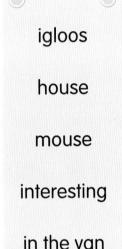

igloos

house

mouse

interesting

in the van

B. **Unscramble and complete the dialogs.**

① A: Look at this!

B: _____
(on / water / the / a / is / house / .)

② A: Is this a floating house?

B: Yes. _____
(people / live / some / in / floating houses / .)

③ A: _____
(interesting / how / !)

B: Yes, it is.

④ A: What are they doing?

B: _____
(selling / fruit / are / boat / the / on / they / .)

Reading Time – Voca

● **Write the words.**

1. _____

2. _____

3. _____

4. _____

5. _____

6. _____

cold

protect

ice

igloo

temperature

extreme

Mongolia & Spain 1

Let's Write

A. Look, choose, and write.

How big is Mongolia?

2 _____

It's in Asia.

1 _____

3 _____

Where is Spain?

4 _____

It's smaller than France.

- It's in Europe.
- How big is Spain?
- Where is Mongolia?
- It's bigger than the Philippines.

B. Write the words.

Africa   Europe   North America   Asia

Mongolia

Kenya

Spain

Canada

_____   _____   _____   _____

C. Choose and write.

1 How _____ is Mongolia?

2 It's _____ than France.

3 _____ is Spain?

4 It's in _____ .

smaller
big
Europe
where

D. Look and write.

Example

A: Where is _Mongolia_ ?

B: It's in _Asia_ .

1

A: Where is _____ ?

B: It's _____ _____ .

2

A: _____ is _____ ?

B: It's _____ _____ .

Mongolia & Spain 2

Let's Write

A. Look, choose, and write.

How far is Mongolia?

① _____

What can I do in Mongolia?

3hrs

② _____

It's very far. It takes about thirteen hours.

③ _____

13hrs

④ _____

You can dance the flamenco.

- How far is Spain?
- You can ride a horse.

- What can I do in Spain?
- It's far. It takes about three hours.

B. Write the words.

 ① _____

 ② _____

 ③ _____

 ④ _____

C. Choose and write.

① How _____ is Mongolia?

② It's far. It _____ about three hours.

③ What can I do in _____?

④ You can _____ the flamenco.

Spain
far
dance
takes

D. Look and write.

Example

A: What can I _do_ in Mongolia?

B: You can _sleep_ in the desert.

①

A: What can I _____ in _____?

B: You can _____ _____ _____.

②

A: What _____ I _____ _____ _____?

B: You _____ _____ _____ _____.

Lesson 13

Leo and Lola Are in Space

Let's Write

A. **Write the words and number the pictures.**

① Leo: Where is Spain?

Lola: It's in _____.

② Leo: How big is Spain?

Lola: It's _____ than Italy.

③ Leo: How _____ is Spain?

Lola: It's far. It takes 13 hours _____.

④ Leo: What can I do in Spain?

Lola: You can _____.

⑤ Leo: _____ go!

Lola: Oh, no!

let's

far

bigger

by plane

Europe

dance the flamenco

How big ...?

... Europe.

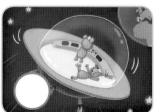

26

B. Unscramble and complete the dialogs.

1 A: Where is Mongolia?

B: _____

(in / it's / Asia / .)

2 A: How big is Mongolia?

B: _____

(the / Philippines / bigger / it's / than / .)

3 A: How far is Mongolia?

B: It's far. _____

(takes / hours / it / three / plane / by / .)

4 A: What can I do in Mongolia?

B: _____

(ride / a / horse / you / can / .)

Reading Time – Voca

● **Write the words.**

1. _____

2.  _____

3. _____

4. _____

5. _____

6. _____

surface

planet

ocean

Earth

continent

huge

Lesson 14 Traditional Costumes

Let's Write

A. Look, choose, and write.

Wow, what are all these?

Excuse me. Can you tell me about it?

① _____

② _____

These are Mongolian costumes.

③ Excuse me. _____

④ _____

They're Mongolian boots.

- It's a Korean wig.
- These are *hanbok*.
- What are all these?
- Can you tell me about them?

B. Write the words.

a Chinese mask   a Mexican hat
Mongolian boots   a Korean wig

①

②

③

④

_____   _____   _____   _____

C. Choose and write.

① Wow, what are all _____?

② These _____ Mongolian boots.

③ Excuse me. Can you _____ me about it?

④ It's a _____.

tell
these
are
Mexican hat

D. Look and write.

Example

A: Can you tell me about _it_?

B: It's a _Chinese_ _mask_.

A: Can you _____ me _____ _____?

B: It's a _____ _____.

A: _____ you _____ _____ about them?

B: They're _____ _____.

Describing People

Let's Write

A. Look, choose, and write.

① _____

Of course.

② _____

You look like a queen.

May I take a picture?

③ _____

How do I look?

④ _____

- You look like a king.
- How do I look?
- Of course.
- May I take a picture?

30

B. Write the words.

king   queen   princess   prince

1  _____

2  _____

3  _____

4  _____

C. Choose and write.

1 May I take a _____ ?

2 Of _____ .

3 How do I _____ ?

4 You look like a _____ .

look
prince
picture
course

D. Look and write.

Example

A: How do I _look_ ?

B: You look like a _queen_ .

1

A: _____ do I _____ ?

B: You _____ _____ a king.

2

A: _____ _____ I _____ ?

B: _____ _____ _____ _____ princess.

You Look Great!

Let's Write

A. Write the words and number the pictures.

1 Nick: You _____ great!

Lola: Thank you.

2 Leo: Wow! What are all _____?

Lola: These are *hanbok*.

3 Leo: _____ I take a picture?

Lola: Of course.

4 Leo: Can you tell me about it? What is it?

Nick: It's _____.

5 Popo: How do I look?

Leo: You look like a _____.

these

princess

may

look

a Mexican hat

Thank you.

B. Unscramble and complete the dialogs.

1 A: _____

(great / you / look / .)

B: Thank you.

2 A: _____

(I / a / take / may / picture / ?)

B: Of course.

3 A: _____

(tell / about / can / you / it / me / ?)

B: It's a Korean wig.

4 A: How do I look?

B: _____

(look / a / like / you / king / .)

Reading Time – Voca

- **Write the words.**

1. _____

2. _____

3. _____

4. _____

5. _____

6. _____

veil

pants

wrap

wear

costume

cloth

A Campaign for Poor Children

Let's Write

A. Look, choose, and write.

1. Mom! Dad! _____ _____

   Oh... they look so sick.

2. _____

   Because they don't have warm clothes.

   Dad! Look at these children.

   Why are they so sick?

3. _____

4. _____ _____

- Oh... they look so sick.
- Why are they so sick?
- Look at these babies.
- Because they don't have enough food.

B. Write the words.

clean water   enough food
warm clothes   enough medicine

1  _____

2  _____

3  _____

4  _____

C. Choose and write.

1 _____ at these babies.

2 They look so _____ .

3 _____ are they so sick?

4 Because they don't have _____ .

look
why
sick
warm clothes

D. Look and write.

Example

A: <u>Why</u> are they so sick?

B: <u>Because</u> they don't have warm clothes.

1

A: _____ are they so _____?

B: _____ they don't have enough _____ .

2

A: _____ _____ they so _____?

B: _____ they don't have _____ _____ .

Helping Children

Let's Write

A. Look, choose, and write.

- We should raise money.
- Mom, what do they need?
- What should we do for them?
- They need clean water and food.

B. Write the words.

write a letter   raise money
knit a hat   send clothes

①  _____

②  _____

③  _____

④  _____

C. Choose and write.

① What do they _____?

② They need _____.

③ What _____ we do for them?

④ We should _____.

should
knit a hat
need
wool hats

D. Look and write.

Example

A: __What__ should we do for them?

B: We __should__ knit a hat.

①

A: What _____ we _____ for them?

B: We _____ _____ a letter.

②

A: _____ _____ we _____ for them?

B: We _____ _____ _____.

What Should We Do for Them?

Let's Write

A. Write the words and number the pictures.

1 Leo: Look at these babies.

Lola: Oh... they look so _____.

2 Popo: Why are they so sick?

Lola: Because they don't have _____ and warm clothes.

3 Nick: What do they _____?

Popo: They need worms and wool hats.

4 Leo: What _____ we do for them?

Lola: We should catch worms.

5 Popo: We should _____!

need

sick

should

knit a hat

enough food

... sick?

B. Unscramble and complete the dialogs.

1 A: Look at these babies.

B: _____
(sick / they / so / look / .)

2 A: Why are they so sick?

B: _____
(don't / medicine / they / enough / have / because / .)

3 A: What do they need?

B: _____
(wool / hats / need / they / .)

4 A: _____
(should / what / do / them / for / we / ?)

B: We should knit a hat.

Reading Time – Voca

- **Write the words.**

1. _____

2. _____

3. _____

4. _____

5. _____

6. _____

increase

knit

help

charity

raise

sell

Memo

ENGLiSH TOWN

BOOK 4

ENGLiSH TOWN BOOK 4

English Town is a spoken English course comprised of a series of 9 books, specifically designed for elementary school students.

- Learning English in a communicative way and in an easy manner
- Focused approach to new words, expressions, and dialogs
- Fun to sing and chant together
- Simple but effective games and activities
- Exciting stories

Components

· Student Book

· Workbook

· Final Test

· Teacher's Guide including teaching resources

· Online (www.ybmenglishtown.com)

  Interactive e-book for teachers and students

  E-learning for self-study

  www.ybmenglishtown.com

YBM